FELTON PRAIRIE

FELTON PRAIRIE

poems

Rodney Nelson

Middle Island Press

2014

ISBN 978-0-6922-6780-6

The cover photo of Elin Viktoria Eriksson (see the
poem on page 18) was provided by Linda Erickson
Schneider and sent by Chris Huntze, to both of
whom thanks are due.

Published by Middle Island Press
PO Box 354
West Union WV 26456

ACKNOWLEDGMENTS

Aire, Anemone Sidecar, Burning River, Dead Drunk Dublin, First Thought, Flutter, High Plains Reader, Jack, Language and Culture, Lowestoft Chronicle, Neon Beam, Ocean Diamond, Ottawa Arts Review, Planet Formerly Known as Earth, Reader's Rejoinder, Sierra Journal, Threshold, Thresholds Literary Journal, Tribe, TSQ, Unlikely Stories, Vanitas, Whistling Shade, White Leaf Journal

CONTENTS

Felton Prairie

ALMANAK

winter you knew had been and that was why
it would have to be
                    Father and Mother
had coats and went unafraid in the snow
that had been on the prairie and would have
to be again
                    you jumped into it from
a riverbank and knew why candles were
lit in the quiet church that evening

spring would come again and again you knew
because it had to
                    Father and Mother
went out in boots to crack the ice of a
mud puddle where you knew a meadowlark
had to follow
                    the prairie dropped clay in
the river and one of twenty children
wore a white carnation to church that day

summer would have to be in green and heat
the way it had been

                        Father and Mother
took you riding on a road you knew that
smelled of animal and would end in wheat
as it all had done

                  hanging prairie grass
let you roll to the river and church you
knew would stand in a fable that morning

fall had been smoke you knew and that was how
it would have to be

                       Father and Mother
went talking among the leaves to burn them
and hurt you in the eye until the light
got weaker

                too long a way down to the
slow water now and the graveyard you knew
would be ringing around the church that night

HANKINSON HILLS

on the bed of the foregone sea
were not too many miles to now
                    in
the time until they made a
roaded bowery of it I
might have hunted wood and water
on the sand delta where a shore
of it had been
                    yet were many
miles to now when I rode among
windrows until the land went up
and greened with tree
                    how whatever
fed the sea had washed out into
hill I did not want to know
                    I
just went hunting until I met
the moment at a chokecherry
in fruit
                    were shelter and shade

                    I
had wood and water of my own
and would have been in still night there
marking the firmamental move
not pass of time
                    taking in the
air again of unbroken earth

                    maybe
                    I stayed
maybe forwent

ABIDING FARMSTEAD

Johan Alm och Marie had come to abide

for an ever within imagination

and I came to bide only minutes on the

driveway of the stead who had not abidden

in any one where too long

        wanting to see

if the fruit of the plums that were wild like me

had ripened full

        that had arrived unbidden

like me at the grove and thriven without a

hand during its human heyday and thrive now

        wild

meant self-planted

        insect- and wind-tended

roving except in body of the seed

to where whatever winged or ran might drop it

        like

me who knew however not to swallow

and I spat right on the drive that none or few

had walked since the landowner relative of

mine quit taking on hands to

            limpiar las

            betabeles

camping them in the ruined

house but newmown yard of Johan och Marie

            a

son of whose had married Ida Hegle

            my grandma's cousin

and farming to the east

had a son that wived a second cousin in

our line

            another heir to Johan och

Marie was the last to bide among the elms

that they indeed had planted and tended

            did

not abide

            but the genealogy song

had a church refrain to hurry them past what

lay outside imagination

            I needed

no hymning

            Abide With Me

that late midday

of a summer beginning to laten and

with a next plomman

            plum

so ready it came

off at my mere tap

        another seed that meant

another generation to drop where John

and Mary elm

        Alm

had come to abide for

an ever and only abode in a way

like the whole grove

        I needed only one more

minute to bide and would be set to run or

wing away to some any one where again

ELIN VIKTORIA ERIKSSON

FIRST COUSIN

TWICE REMOVED

1883–99

the autumn had been due her and come
but was retreating to the river
on which it would leave

she watched it tint
the water that it drifted into
and keep on moving

at the farmhouse
they were putting a match to the wick
in midafternoon

she might have gone
a mile with the river and seen the

other family

that had no room
to keep the youngest in but would want
her again someday

how it had been
in Nora bergsförsamling until
Mama Stina died

but now she gave
the work and company of her to
a foster hemma

everyone
knew that Elin Viktoria was
not an orphan kid

she could turn all
they wanted her to do on the farm

into a polka

        the autumn had
been and soon the river it took would
bring her fifteenth year

        and it did but
Elin would not be due to watch the
next one come or drift

        the window glass
of an empty bedroom would break and
a family would nest in the wall

DIMENSION

good work I did in the days would
mitigate the onrush effect
of them I had hoped
                what I made
and left would slow them down even
though time of nothing done I knew
had gone the same way
                I shall leave
my rot at the end of me and
not of the dimension I move
in that moves in and around me
                the
work I do will remain a
minute more as the days run on

TOWARD THE EDGE

old times have ended

he declaimed on Labor

Day nineteen fifty-three or fifty-three years

ago now

old times

he did not acclaim

have

ended

baldpate in a wooden chair they had

taken outside for the clan gathering

a

Norwidgeon in America

my aging

unmoneyed lawyer politician granddad

as my drunk dad and uncle rassled on the

yard of what had been a farmstead

the crickets

had anything to add but I went hiding

in the watcher woods and was not an adult

schizophrenic

only a kid

only this

morning we were in

old times

I might have thought

now it is too late

for an old-time fight

who

had just begun to pluck the bowstring and would

have to learn draw and aim in a country of

more and more chairiot traffic toward the

edge of arcuarius

had not sweat or bled

HEADING NORTH

I am turning right in a now that could be then
from North Dakota forty-six onto county
seventeen and cannot see the elevator
and the water tower of the town you may or
may not live in even though it is only nine
miles away

       I have an ache but not from looking
at the rich late-summer green in the ditches and
the bean fields' saffron nor is it entirely
the lack of you

       I do not expect or need to
spot the town either that any one tree claim to
the north may be hiding

       horizon and sky meet
at my own level and I was a prairie kid
to whom unlimited vacancy gave comfort
but hurt and am one now and know that where you may
or may not live will edge into view

       that my ache
is the plangent effect of a beauty I do

not want to name any more than the migrant hawk

meeting me minutes ago would

      he too is sky

and prairie

      an embodiment of the longing

and minutes earlier he might have seen you in

the town that now or then is moving up to me

SEPTEMBRIAN

between the public wall and walk the garden
is overweighed
       the stalks do not hold up what
they were meant to carry and lie bent among
greens that darken the half shade
       an attitude
of thrown-out surfeit but not of leavings from
dinner
       maybe from salad in
       the kitchen
good nontable scraps that would have to be chewn
       a
plant has a name and it means nothing to
any knower that has not grown up with it
       to
learn funkia only in order to
write the word is to misguide
       well
      the public
gardener must have thought so
      there are no signs

REED SOLO

hawk over empty field had made a
one-bird day in autumn heat that led
or did it to the next of hard cold
wind and remoter valley and clouds
of which weathermen had foretold were
rolling in or would have been were that
site any more than an unmarked way
point like every other with clouds
rolling through not in nor was the one
blue heron of the day heading to
a river that moved just to direct
him on toward a roost night in which
were anything to call or even
begin to he would only listen

VILLAGE GREEN

I walked in sun in the moon
when a calf grows hair but not
that calf

                    ptecila

          I mean

          raw dark one
and were some dry
poplar leaves on the ground of
the mock neighborhood

          were mock
hummocks on real prairie that
men had made green

          no manner
of calf in this lea

          what would

                    Pasternak
have made of the
huge driveways and fairways

          an
electric baldachin cart
I thought

                    all drapes were pulled to
keep out the sun or to keep
in what he would not have known

                        moon when, *et seq.*:   September
                        ptecila: junior bison (Lakota)

YOUR COUNTRY

wide trail
                    a foot avenue
rounding the lake in woods of
green and once-green leaf

                              autumn
not quite in the sky or here
only an intent
                    the scent
of old wet vegetable
went with obliquity yet
a crow was heard
                    staccato
in woods that would have muffled
it a month ago
                    had not
much other calling in them
                    were hollowed
                    now

                              rain

                    only
an aspergillum and one
minute of sun
                    enough to
undo a crow's obloquy

WHITE ASTERS

at the coming of fall and the new moon
they were out already by the river
         the distant white
light in the dim of their
leaves seemed unaccountable
         they were out
on the country driveway
         pricks of flower
chilling the ground thicket under the tree
row
         uncountable
         with a name you would
have had to say below a whisper and
did not
         you were even more among them
now
         silenter
         whiter
         farther away

FIRST OF AUTUMN

autumn nineteen eighty-seven I picked
and kept a turned oak leaf in a notebook
        had written
                  from wholesaler to hermit
in regard to some what I do not know
but it would have been a tree in an old
river meadow that grew it
        I liked the
acres one relative of mine had been
fostered on where no one at all had lived
in a half century
        was yet to learn
their harder history
        in that June of
my own an old friend I no longer knew
had shot and hanged himself
        who had been the
                original hippie
introduced me
        to
           On the Road

and
                marijuana which
smelled like asthma powder burning
                he had
found work as a greeting-card wholesaler
and maybe my note meant that I who had
started out like that had gone another
way
                I had not written it down at the
time nor in August when my uncle died
                        wholesale-retail merchant
and not too old
                I must have put it in
                more around the
first of autumn
                the same turn nineteen years
on today yet the brown of the leaf means
it would have turned later and it has kept
brown from when I walked to the meadow to
the now of my table and morning rain
                while
I may have turned from wholesale man to
a hermit in the heartwood of the word

eighty-seven I took this leaf
offa oak tree southa town
I wrote me a note or something
but I cant figgert out now

ya it was in the year that George
hung himself too I recall
an someone borrowed him a gun
so he shot himself as well

ya Orville he died that summer
couple months later dint he
an he been sick but I might have
to look up that date an see

wisht I knew what itted meant on
that note I wrote to me too
even if you got a oak heart
I guess itll crack on you

PRAELUDIUM

cold windstorm made a hurrying
of the park in the air mainly
so little remained to whick or
        spin
men that had mown the fall leaves
would wait to take what came down now
        a branch or more
many squirrels
were hunching together on a
dry bare patch around one oak
        tails
kinked low in the hurry
        might have
been adding to and might have been
removing
        were gray
        whatever
wanted to refuge in sunlight
had to stay out of the main air

FALL DAY

great heron working alone at a roadside pond
where hill and lake began and the farmed fields were low
        had remained to the too-much north

        in the too-much
warmth of October one it seemed not to matter
that sumac were in full red and the milkweed in
full seed when green marked the woods along with yellow

        Canada geese
lay over at what had been one
man's lake refuge and needed no hurry now or
wayleave
        some other would be hunted and it did
not seem to matter on a day in full sun that
everything other or not was dying
        would
not have mattered indeed because all days were fall
days and like too-ripe apples on the earth
        werc good

TWO OCTOBER

afternoon had to get late to reach perfection
the summer to close
        that yellow leaf to quit a
tree's height moving down on blue in hard dry wind
           green
and warm remaining would have meant day forever
a cling of too much light and the wrens' moment in
it
        what was had to go
        be remembered
           to
           reach
accord in the dimming and get taken away

PRAIRIE WATERS IN FALL

midget dandelion in color
                    only one
            an inadequate-sun
            emblem
nonnative grass
in color too of June without proclivity
                    bluestem
turning sable out on the open flat

osprey intending right over the part-unleaved
gallery woods
                    no wing work
            only wing
            close-hauled
athwart a wind out of its wanted direction
                    the eyes
on what in the inadequate river

hunting what away from main waters

                              not Procne

                    not Philomena

                    no

          a migrant from the sub-

          arctic

                              white underfeather

          on a tack too west

not late autumn but prereckoning north
wind in the river grove which could not run
with it
      had to buckle
      cede what orange
and other leaf remained
      wind that moved the
            Raum zwischen
            den Fingern
      in a way you
      would not have felt a week ago
            Gustav
            Vigeland
imagined her
            Camilla
            Collett
      in it
            kvinnesakens store
            pionér
      who had written
            det blåser

en kald vind

mot enker i

dette land

you have seen a photo of the sculpted

widow holding

sjalet samlet

rundt seg

a Norwegian park

but in this one now

a statued gray woodchuck at its hole not

chancing to move

movement only among

weed and orange and other ceded leaf

Raum, et seq.	space between the fingers (from Peter Handke's *Mein Jahr in der Niemandsbucht*)
Gustav Vigeland	(1869–1943) Norwegian sculptor
Camilla Collett	(1813–95) Norwegian writer
kvinnesakens, et seq.	great pioneer feminist
det blåser, et seq.	it is a cold wind blowing on the widows of this country
sjalet, et seq.	the shawl gathered round her

FELTON PRAIRIE

FOR ELIZABETH LYNCH

yellow butterflies

      some white

            were few

at the gravel edge of your prairie

not yet a month into autumn

          one

unimagined vagrant magpie yawed

on the hunt stick pile of a butcher

bird

      little wind would have carried the

ditch smoke over only now

not then

      crickets

          not many either

      made more

than they took of a silence you would

have known on farmed or unfarmed prairie

      you

had the hum of it within you

GRAFFITO 1907

an old man's love is pitiful
to no one's observation more
than to his trained and wintered own

each hieing moment takes away
from what he has to give and brings
the end of him in clearer sight

yet moments are a home to him
and he may find reflowering
in the now or again of them

it might have been a hunting
or hunted insect that twirled
no more than half a moment
into window view and could
not have been no not even in
the sun warmth
               might have been a
town sparrow that had its own
at work or play though what kind
of play it would have been at
in the midfall was hard to
imagine
               had to have been
a leaf that had gotten caught
on air surf and put in mock-
celebratory motion
as if to invoke even
lighter flurrying to come

DOLDRUM TIME

gray and gray-white flurr of junco into the
waiting grove and tinier bird already
up
        would not have needed crown or king in its
        name
            gold dot
        beelike attention to the tree

much leaf down and should have been more and the re-
planted grass have quit but no cold to laten
the year
        leather smell too rife
        in the damp grove
            giant willow
        on the bank too thick of green

what moved with me on the prairie would not turn
into a call or a hug
                resolve that way
yet the look of midoctober had thistle
in flower about it and even I hung
onto some
                           great light and heat
                           and dry and wet
                had already been so
how could its purple
have gone on to the attraction of who knew
or the expression of what
                I had come through
my own high season
                           the braying and breeding
                           and given and taken hurt
                known enough salt
water and mountain to get me home so how
could any bloom have remained
                attracting whom
                expressing what

        maybe

it was due to its

outliving of June that a weed flowered now

maybe I had made it through my time only

to call on the prairie in autumn

        touch it

LATER TIME IN A STATE PARK

outer sumac had a remnant patch
of vermilion and the grove looked
reseda with an overmuch green
in what still hung even the downed and
I did not know the calling I heard
beyond it that my arrival had
started but did know the takeover
pointed cry of a red-tail hawk and
saw him wheeling away to further
the unknown call into more daylight
it might have seemed and now were redpoll
in the open too to think about

THRUDVANG

MIGRANTS' STOPOVER

high mild north wind had been around
the county taking leaf and as
I walked in where the hilly drive
had use to go I did not think
to see any at the onetime
farmstead
        no blowing today and
an easy ocher light even
toward noon on faded tall-grass
acreage that dropped away to
the grove he had lived in
             I heard
them at the time I saw the one
gold height of a poplar among
naked oak next to an only
remembered garden site
        a black-
        bird shivaree
            red-wing

                    Brewer's

                cowbird and grackle

out of that

direction though I did not quite

get what they were until I had

edged up in the underwood and

unkept woods they had set all in

motion

                a migrant-flock music

                a day stopover

at what the

old man had given them

                        workmen

                had come to remove

                the last mark

                of him but a rusty pail and

                a crock shard

no motion around

just quiet and late October

and my father might have liked this

MORE STUDY

I saw a bird that would not
have been there
             preying
             white

                        more
than twenty of it and each
in an own low wheeling scan
of the autumned earth among
the potholes of which I had
met a garter snake and a
muskrat

                        hunter
                        no gull

             with
dark neb hook the wing technique
of a peregrine
             bird that
would not have been wheeling out
over this brown wetland in
day warmth
             would have been in the

right migratory lane its

route from the nesting region

to the wintering

                I saw

a bird that would not have been

there had it known every-

thing I knew

          not have flaunted

its black wing patch

                I saw

     a

     bird

that may need more study

NOT THIS FALL

I walked mainly into a northwest wind out of
Canadian plain that brought no warm to this one
and got to the waned-out farmstead where bunting were
the expected activity in midautumn
        I watched them
favor mainly naked plum thicket
along the drive and had to content my eye with
the gray of them and of today until the honk
              or
a part honk only
        they were southwestering
athwart the wind at three or so hundred feet up
and black on the sky
           silent
        a ravine cut through
the stead that rain might have filled of which the old point
gander had memory so known how to vector
then seen me turn where water did not wait and honked
to the vee
          not this fall
      evacuating on

TO THE SWEDE MIGRATION

Eden land that had to have been awaited you on
a northwest prairie and the Eden river that might
have given you a name
            you freighted the word along
of native bliss country to plant again in a new
wild-flowery Sharon
            the bell of testimony
            revelation
            good work
with it to ring up the sun
that would enlight the ending day and you had and would
have no other in which to enunciate beauty
            what shone
            in May were not just
                    blommor uti dalen
but lily in valley of chapter and verse and when
you hurt for home would conjoin in a hymn that let the
dark and snow away
            know that come one pearl evening
you would go to death as to devotion
                    reawake

           in native summer bliss

wood you worked and rock you picked

remain on your Eden farmstead next to the vineyard

of your bibliolatry

           the word continues to

ring out from New Joppa to New Carmel trying

to reach you wherever you went

                  not in your boneyard

blommor uti dalen   valley flowers

GOLDENING

between dike and river the color in willow
hung on in the lull of a warm not summery
day
            hip-high dock weed kept some too
            russet that in
the clarity of afternoon seemed to golden
and invite the watcher but to what
            a student
crow worked at the river edge to the chivvying
of a parent
            he might not have wanted to leave
            for it to either
                    der Tag ist süss und ladet
                    eïn
his argument might have run who knew only
summer
            nothing of any fadeaway or end
            no
current even showed and smoke would have gone straight
up and been reflected
            too late
            the autumn for

that was over and olden crows and olden men

were ready to yield to winter not this

        goldened

day of no motion that invited them to what

The day is sweet and inviting.
           —Wilhelm Lehmann

WIDOW'S NEW HOME

her kitchen view at the nine-acre farmstead
would not have been different
           hard green pasture
           in continual autumn
no snow sheet yet
to wind it in only here a huge window
on the bright gray of midmorning which seemed to
amplify day
           point it
but she did not hurt
thinking of the man that had gone to an earned
relaxation in another lawn
might do
that too
           here in the home
           they had made for rest
might have to with widowhood continuing
the chance of finding any next to him not
good with every day or night hanging on
longer the slower it had come
           now time would

amplify beyond end point

she would get to

eternity at this high window

maybe

UNTIRING LIGHT

no more yellow autumn
        into gray fall now
but warm with a luxus of light that
time cannot impoverish
        a day fulfilled
at noon and I am walking it on
the river path anyway
        I was thinking
of travel when I came of how to
get my mind through the dim heavy months until
I could
        but the dead hanging willow
leaves have no weight
        the sun all among them would
not have to be and might as well make
them reflect
        the idiot river working
north into an early freezeup will
drudge to Winnipeg at its own any rate
        I
am not waiting

         my journey has
always been on and I do not even have
to know the point that I have moved to
                no
the moment is comportable enough
a moment of warm only tired
grass untiring light and
            I abound in it

NEVER AT HOME

a gull or two or three hauling east
up in the mild November sky
are on the whitherward of almost
every cloud that I have watched
but I would not want to follow them
                wing through
                                Duluth
                                Québec
                                Glasgow
                                Trondheim
in a sting of bright cold rain
                they
seem to be going all home
to a what that is I would not know
                it
may be hauling them instead
toward the retreating horizon
                I
do not have to go their way
who know that wherever I might have
stopped the horizon would remain

even with my taking off again

to another same some other

looking on

Chadron

Pueblo

Gallup

Tucson

a trump of sun and rock

never

at home but in the winging

SWEDE GRAVEYARD

their waiting continued on a prairie knoll
not quite at the river with unmighty guest
fir around that had no winging in them and
a few of the markers added dull pink to
a rich autumn monochrome
                  the noonlight had
neither wind nor cloud and would have invited
meditation but I had come only to
look at two of the family names and ask
about the red glow in me that they had known
and died of
                  the woman in the directest
hard way
                            why won't it quit Emma
                            tell me Pär
not having to wait on an answer with them
I went out to a grove to which no named one
had homed in more than a hundred fifteen years
and met some winging and color there
                  junco
                  chickadee
                  jay

a dandelion or two

in anachronic live grass and in open

weedy patches a dotting of wild-rose hip

READY AGAIN

three times around the calendar had
been enough for the old packman to
cut and leave any territory
who would get no more than once around
the clock in all

                    but midway through a
                    gig I met someone of autumn lake
                    and flower and went on a splurge in
                    poetry the counting forgotten

the clock that should have said nine thirty
read nine and the calendar when he
looked had not moved beyond a nine-month
point from the end the both running down
or out before the packman

           and when

                    she did not want my words anymore
                    I heard a ticking the turn of a
                    page and had to ready me again
                    to leave for other territory

ROUTE

I had been let into
            not doomed to
the world with Fargo as porte cochère
let in to climb on the stone highland
to the edge of great water and woods
            in time I
went back that way to the
very porte the gate to age and it
was a trapdoor now but it let
            did
            not doom me
to fall through country of
extravagant green and blue and white

QUIET TUESDAY

twelfth moon did not show through or on

Tuesday following it which marked

the nativity of who had

arrived messianic without

army or crown or a mind to

hail the tribes in and refound the

temple yet with mojo beyond

a written word

        in this neck of

winter it warmed though no one tried

to do a rendition of The

Nut Carol at the park's snowy

belvedere and imagining

what river would have sounded like

only made the day quieter

WHAT CHANCE

Fergus Falls in memory an ache toward the human
toward Madeline playing cello in black and Judith
who would not wait at eighteen and Elle at thirty-four
I had hurt and taken to talk-therapy next to a
dry park in afternoon heat
        the human meant women then
and in the town was beauty of a round lake and the elms
and the Otter Tail but an old man my dad died on its
edge in summer too who had let me use even rename
the hidden patchy woods farm he owned and I ached toward
the history he meant
        when I dreamed black oak or black-oak
groves of Minnesota into poem I had Fergus
Falls in memory an ache toward the romantic
not yet come to a view that would wipe the romance of being
humanity out would see it as conflagration and
the planet's dried-up end
        in the meantime which is all I
have however I want to walk in Fergus again and
imagine what a Celt wordman would have made of the name
of it what chance

a one more oak-grove dream might have hoping

that the head of the Red Branch kings be on his feet in May

AT THE GRANDPARENTS'

the other kid and the dog and I
would run into a daze of July
and the woods' burdock on the river

or only around the farmstead grove
or out in heat-choked wheated prairie
to wade and hop in the flax beyond

we needed the leash of a mere word
and would run a mosquito gauntlet
to the yard in time for evening

one night I told the dog goodbye and
he jumped and yipped to say it and more
and he went down in early winter

the kid told me the same and more with

his look no talk and he went under
a drifting truck in another snow

neither kid nor dog wanted mourning
and the more they had needed to say
was keep on running to the river

THAT DAY

I came to the town I knew as it would have
been without me
       the lake the half-snag willow
where egret had built had nothing in them and
the worn-out green of October when I looked
drew away
       a wisp of the feeling I had
clutched at in word met me downtown to which I
followed and no one could see me there
               human
movement that had seemed avian
             balletic
      in July
was puppetlike now and where it
went on I did not go not even into
a room I might have found vacant
       I was half
            ghost
already in a town without me had
no more than that day to put a word on it

LAURA

she had married without a crown of myrtle
in winter but when the genealogy
came to May light the grove a mile away was
Laura who had not been out only dead and
unknown to me like many on the Jansson
prairie
            I could see her in the reaching high
of cottonwood as in the wedding photo
and saw to the east the willowed farmyard of
an uncle that had worked and lusted to death
at an earlier Maytime
                        Alice had played
the ukulele and been even more the
lovely sister and not lived to have any
crown at all
            another Jansson of photo
to enter my memory nine years ago
and now is a walk on the road again and
they of the names that made me will not return
to the prairie
                    will be the cottonwood and

willow I see
in every catkin May

.

HOLD OF THE PASSED

you watched it from older country and went
and from here too as I would do in time
and you went again
                    had me with you to
watch it from High Point until was nothing
but sign in it then you came as I in
time would do
                    came back to more a sky than
any and to pass not go
                              I am here
taking more a March wind than Seattle
or older country would know and am not
gone but have your words with me on a road
or avenue
                    you are passed
                not gone and
I am here with you and wind watching sky
that may have no more sign in it for me

DEPOT PLAZA

could not have been more familiar
the hot west wind

           I had lived downtown
as a hurrying kid and sat at
a fountain now that had come later

I knew the brick on the other side
of the avenue
          not this linden
      flowering

but a train came by in
the old hurry and away it went

I WANTED AGRIMONY

I wanted agrimony
so I went between row on
row of unripe bean and a
field where wind was moving
in tall green wheat
           the yellow
flowers were out I thought and
the sun would lead me hunting
to ditch and ravine so I
did not wait in the grove
and listen for a hawk kill

I wanted agrimony
a cocklebur in the mind

AT THE TABLE

you would rather have no rain than warm
but will await
            the clearing that is
not here will come
                        the prairie around
turn light in a way that is not yet

you would not want to be over there
in the clearing
            will await at an
oaken table
                        the window open
until it is warm without raining

QUICK OUT

I did not see what dropped with a grunt
of both alarm and resignation
or the hitting hawk outside the grove

were many hidden known bones of man
and animal here many hidden
and not and now would be a few more

a quiet intermitted the field
work in the high summer and let me
hear what the prey had time to give out

I did not see the hawk come or hit
and drop it but will not have to be
at the farm to relive that one grunt

SIGN OF WHAT

moon of middle summer too low
in the south

                        mead moon in the old
            north time and after

                    to me the
sign of what I tend to forget
when I am working

                  I think of
           a name and the moon is higher

FARTHER ONTARIO

I am a loon at a lake
rather on one but moon is
up to remind how alone
I am
         having no moon made
the dark full and now where I
am is not and I want to
dive
         there is a moan in it
but I am more a loon than
alone or at some degree
of mere human loneliness
                  no
one can be too loonly

TERMS AND CONDITIONS

view of dirigible from High Point
                    one white cloud
          wrote an end on the blue
to the term in Seattle that had
not been meant to go on

                    I am old
          where we came to begin the next and
cloud and the blue are the same without
a dirigible

                    I did not want
          to stay or get away or return
to North Dakota and looking up
was contentment

                    Seattle would not
          be home they told one another

and me and where we came I started

looking down

        the prairie

    looking back

what knew me turning into earth I

knew and the term in North Dakota

was meant to go on and on

        they said

    but not that it would not have an end

I am here for an intended term

writing it out

    with fear insurance

COUNTRY ELEGY

by Ron Winkler

translated from the German

this day is radioing
over the wind channel.

*

in the wheat fields the stalks of devotion
are gaining currency.

*

pollen airing itself over the country:
gratuit et libre.

*

blossoms are directly
outsourcing their aromas.

*

solo gusts stir knotted shrubbery
to branch into hymn.

*

in many a harebell
church initiatives are swinging.

*

cats in their own
world as ever.

*

the birds are overruled. they end
the day in silent mode.

*

around midnight the regional anthem
of the pond frogs.

LÄNDLICHE ELEGIE

das Sendegerät dieses Tages
ist auf den Windkanal eingestellt.

*

in den Weizenfeldern gewinnen
Andachtshalme an Geltung.

*

über dem Land Pollenverschickung,
gratuit et libre.

*

unverblümt lagern Blüten
ihre Aromen aus.

*

einzelne Böen animieren knorrige Sträucher

zu verästelten Hymnen.

*

in manchen Glockenblumen
schwingen Kirchenversuche.

*

die Katzen unverändert
per Sie mit ihrer Umgebung.

*

die Vogel sind überstimmt. sie beschliessen
den Tag im *silent mode*.

*

um Mitternacht die Regionalhymne
der Frösche am Teich.

LAMMAS

down the river and along it a
calm outswell of green in the heat blur
and midday perfection

        elder and
basswood have waited to join to make
an own memorial depiction
during this sun height

        even no wind to
mar the mastery of what fathered
you and will grant the harvest loaf in
a minute or week

        but it is late
midday and you detect in the bank
the poverty of gray November
that a cutting wind will have let out

LAX MOMENTUM

slough a part of a meandering indentation
in the flat grass- now cropland then at the farmstead a
lower part of it and in wet months an overgrown
lough then cordgrass and cocklebur at an outlet of
the leaving sometime drain way

                 no run on this dog day
and in the cottonwooded slough only hard black earth
to mark the water lie of early June and when you
turn to the sky you need no lamasery teaching
relaxation to know a mind at ease will not be
other than kind

              but crossing the outlet north you know
a change of land and air that you will see the fleeing
dark young hawk before you even look at its watch tree
and not worry to put a name on what is all nerve
homing for a remote grove in neither Sichuan
nor Scituate and dwindling with a mere cloud or two
into another part of the day's lax momentum

PILGRIMS

FOR WARREN WILLIAMS

if we had not gone and ridden the way from
Tamaulipas to Tamalpaís we
might never have known earth in February

staying in our native winter country
would have made what so much better for whom as
we knew when we went and took that right turn south

but we were the ones de Crèvecoeur had written
about and we meant to leave even though it
put hurt on the many and more not dreaming

it was our term in variegated
February and the quick scent of bay and
oleander and paloverde and warm

salt sand that let us come back in undue or
due time where men do not abide without a
mind to the tick of living earth under snow

we ride the way from Tolna to Tioga
who once went popping a quirk in Sonoma
and know what the pilgrim worms are at down there

YOUNG COUSIN STAN

he had the front wheel of a truck coming
and it got him in the neck when he fell
out on an iced country road
        he and the
ground met the weight of what had been coming
and no one other would have done
        both sky
and church were hard too on the funeral
winter morning and the young men that bore
his pall did not want it trucked away
        were
raring to follow but only he had
driven out to that road that time and each
of them had another front wheel coming

KNOWN REACH

it might have been Leeds we met in
or some other city north enough
to dim at midday when a cloud
lay over
                              I had said one word and
you were of utter mind to be
this summer latening time with me
                              how we went
or wound up at a
South Dakota mountain I did not
have to know when I woke to your
trim nakedness
                              we were already
quenched it seemed but you fed me choc-
olate cake with love and let me use
your toothbrush
                              I did not have one
must not have dared to plan or to pack
even though the cabin was mine
and we had arrived in my maroon
sedan

you were off alone to

climb the mountain which did not deso-

late me nor did I wonder why

I a trekking man had not gone too

only watched you through the window

                              you had an

animal in your arms

a cat maybe not that it meant

anything

                                 what mattered was to load

the sedan then drive to the top

surprise you

                              or not in that we had

agreed without a word I would

                            what meant was

a love too good to be

talkative we could trust in to

lengthen a moment beyond known reach

                            I started

up to where I would

meet you

                            have not reached it yet but I

know who you were and you know me

MY PLACE

our purpose is to govern ourselves with one eye
dreaming and one on the difficult balance at hand.

George Evans

we would be cold into bed a
thick foam pad on the rug
                narrow but good
you would watch me ease up out of
it and hear my knee crack when I stretched
                in
a room an apartment with no tele-
vision only the memory of a
reader's pipe smoke
                would you look with
sorrow at the predawn luminescence
in my window or would you vault
to the day
                your body's glad prime too much
for any second thinking no

matter that the man of your moment
               might
not last it
               I would be making
antioxidant green tea not a meal
would take my antihyperten-
sive medication later
               once we had
done our rollick out in some
light field of green or snow having had not
much choice but to live in and for
the now
               once I had returned on my own
to the neighborhood of the old

BIRTHNIGHT

on the road of unwritten saga
there will have to be a lake that no one
has recorded or even half known
               migrant pelicans
will have granted it
to many a loon and a midnight
that may not expect you
               no matter that
you will walk up to the unfinished
cabin of who wanted to write the place
whom the dim lake would have recognized
               and must have
run or been run away on
that same road
               must have come as you will
to a silence now folding in again
many a night bird joining it when
you do put your own hand to the saga

PATH

thick dark June leaves crowding in
on the river bypath where
it has a turn are lovely
and I know of words that would
make the noon of them chitter
and be unending for you
but I do not have any
that would tell how much I miss
your unafraid look or how
absent you are on the path

WHERE YOU ARE

I am of the day and I want to
stay in it but maybe the night is
where you are
              the only medium
of communion that we have had
between eleven and half past
              if
dream had been experience then one
year ago we lay at the foot of
a stone mountain and last night in a
condo of yours in the Mother Lode
              you
were a summiter then
              now had
freckled breasts
              a dream however is
the work of mind without refinement
              nonart
              nonempirical
I have
thought but maybe it is a way to
call or call on each other in your

only medium too when a wak-
ing attempt between eleven and
eleven thirty does not go through

PRAIRIE WETLAND

trail went around on the hummocky earth and
around and even without a hiding tree
he had a right approach and needed not have
flushed the heron he had not known of but a
green heron hove up loud out of the reed bed
circling

        that same June day he went around in
a public room and waited half-hidden to
talk with a known right woman he could see but
she did not turn and moved away and out which
made a hunter alien of him who had
not been going around to flush anyone

YOUR OWN

you might have seen me in your town
at the full moon
                    either June or
                    May
you might have driven around
the lake of the cormorant tree
while I was gandering
                            but not
                            at night
and you would have picked out
my big straw hat as I got to
the library
                    have gone to a
                    window
I know I reached the door
and earlier the tree
                            in May
                            or June
I could see every
detail of green in your town and
smell the heat

I had to

be there

yet have not been at any time

of the moon in June or May and

to see me you would have had to

do the bilocating

your own

Other Middle Island Press titles by Rodney Nelson are available via Amazon.com and the Middle Island Press website.

Fargo (2014)

ISBN 978-1-4951-0352-0

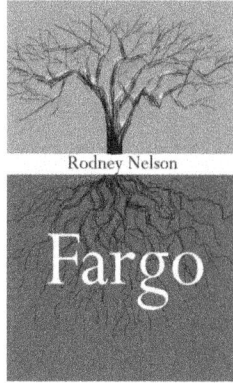

Sighting the Flood (2013)

ISBN 978-1-4675-7626-0

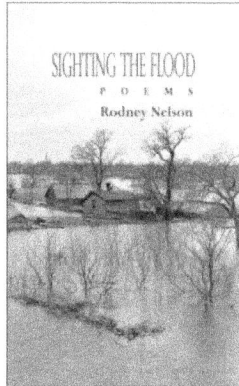

Bog Light (2013)

ISBN 978-1-4675-6739-8

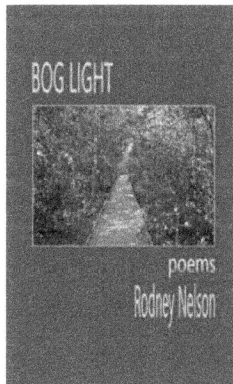

www.ingramcontent.com/pod-product-compliance
Lightning Source LLC
Chambersburg PA
CBHW030957090426
42737CB00007B/572